This Planner belongs to :

_____

_____

Table of content

Before you read this Planner

Personal details

Emergency contacts

Medical information-Medications

Medical information-Doctor's information and contact

Medical information-My view on life support

Financial information-Bank account

Financial information-Safe deposit Box details

Financial information- Debit/credit details

Financial information - Dept/Loan/Mortgages

Insurance details

Property holdings

Caring for children and others who depend on me

Caring for my pets

Internet information (accounts, e-mails, profiles...)

Who has possession of my last will and testament

Recommendations for my funeral

Letters for loved ones

Apologies

Last words

Highlights of my life

Extra notes

Printed in Great Britain
by Amazon

59710181R00057